Bring me Sunshine

Bring Me Sunshine

Poems by

Margie Westmoreland

Rising Hope Publishing Hamilton, Mississippi

Photos credits: All images are original images by Margie Westmoreland

Library of Congress Control Number: 2026902532

ISBN: 979-8-218-83414-2 (paperback)
FIRST EDITION

Content

BRIGHTER DAYS

INTO THE LIGHT

Dedication

For my sons, the anchors of my focus and the source of my strength through every trial, every tribulation, and every triumph.

"Without the love of family, a person stands alone, walks alone, and dies alone." - Margie Westmoreland

Introduction

The darkest days in our lives often feel endless. In those moments, everything seems lost, and hope feels unreachable. It wasn't until later in life that I came to understand what depression truly was—and how to begin healing from it. Troubling times can leave a person in a debilitated state of body and mind, unable to imagine a future or seek solutions.

This book begins in the shadows, where pain and confusion reign. It then moves through the quiet acceptance of circumstances, and finally toward a deeper understanding of what it means to rise above a life that was never ideal.

My goal is to offer you a glimpse into my resilient spirit, in hopes that you'll discover your own strength. Because once healing begins, the light of hope becomes easier to see—and with it, the promise of a better life waiting just beyond the darkness.

The Need for Sunshine

Bring me my Sunshine
for my dark life needs the light,
and my soul, the warmth.

* My first poem, written when I was 13. I did not realize how much darkness would come into my life and how that would shape who I was to become.

In the Darkness

Don't Cry For Me

Tried to live in your world, but I didn't fit.
There in the room so dimly lit,
contemplating the end of my misery.
No sadness, just a goodbye.
Don't try to understand the why.
Save your tears, and you don't cry.
My pain and anguish have all ceased.
No more remorseful thoughts or insecurities.
Couldn't quiet the voices in my head,
the ones that pushed me over the edge.
My agony wasn't about what you did or didn't do,
but rather the struggle I was going through.
Accept that I no longer live in this torturous state.
Whatever the reason, this was my unfortunate fate.
Though now gone from the physical world, and life
may seem unfair.
I will forever reside in your heart if you keep me there.

*** *When people lose hope, it's about the person's internal struggles, not about anyone else's actions. We try to understand why it happened, but at the time it was the only solution this person thought they had. Suicidal ideation can happen to anyone. If you need help overcoming your depression and suicidal thoughts, seek help, call the national hotline 988, pray, but don't battle this alone. Stay, don't let it be your end.*

Alone in my World

I am alone, isolated from the cold world outside,
seeking solace within my realm where I reside,
that pleasant solitary place.

I am alone amongst a sea of people, where only
pleasantries exist but nothing of substance.
I am an ambiguous wanderer without a destination
through life, most unaware of my existence.

I wear no more than a smile, a facade, to hide the
underlying chaos that is my life,
hiding the river of tears I've cried.

They cannot see the anguish buried deep inside.
They mustn't, or they dare break down the walls I have
worked tirelessly to build
over a lifetime of distress.

If only there were a glimmer of hope and happiness,
in this world so lost with such carelessness.
How I yearn to find a peaceful moment to quiet the
demons of the past,
and silence the voices of deceit and regret.

Instead, those horrid memories haunt me and never let
me forget.
Is there a future, or am I doomed to be forever alone in
my world?

Days of Winter Sorrow

Feels like I came here to die in this snow-covered abyss,
where my spirit is diminished—crushed into a void of
nothingness.
My passion for life slowly and cruelly extinguished.
My love for all things is dying, soon to be vanquished.
Even my faith is fading and diminishing like a long-ago
memory.
No longer caring about my existence or my strength, I
find only misery.
Here in the darkness, I exhaust my last ounce of hope
and willpower.
There are no family or friends to support me in this
desperate hour.
Dead even though still breathing, my soul still
unreleased.
Being dead while still alive is worse than actually being
deceased.
For in the ground, no one can hurt you; there are no
worries or cares—
There's just nothing, not even unspoken prayers.

No Escape, No Safe Place

The darkness has invaded my hollowed space,
like a black veil that hides my face.
I find no sanctuary from the evils that dwell.
I am left with no way to escape this destined hell.
These dark shadows descend in full disguise,
to chase away the sunlight from my skies.
I am trapped in a chamber of endless gloom,
a captive soul sealed in this forgotten room.
No whisper, no sound, just despair's cold breath,
lingering, taunting—in love with death.
In silence, I lie motionless, cold and bare—
my heart once whole, is now beyond repair.

Unaffected

Whose eyes have not yet cried
In the stillness of the night,
As the moon's light cascades,
Upon the moistened tear-drenched face?

Words of wisdom fall upon deaf ears;
The mass of voices speaking, make it
Difficult to discern what's needed or
What's true.

Moving toward the light seems
A million miles away,
so distant, so far out of reach,
Making it safer to stay in the darkness.

Can any one soul be truly
Unaffected by the grim
Realities that exist in the world?

The Prisoner in My Room

Locked away within the silent, opaque walls, the
prisoner is trapped.
The deafening quiet erodes the joy of a once gleeful
soul,
who watches and wonders as each teardrop falls.
Once again, the lowly being is exasperated by life, while
the hours and minutes tick sluggishly by
and the day begrudgingly succumbs to the dreary night.
Here in the cell, darkness extinguishes the iridescent
light and
the outside world ceases to exist.
The prisoner dare not be visited or even missed,
for the walled existence is all that is known.
In the shadows, the solitary human paces alone
across the creaky floors, with no destination
other than restless movement—
all while the invading enemy steals the normalcy from
this desperate soul,
adding to the confusion of the pleasures denied.
This frail creature is still searching for a connection—an
awakening from the horrid nightmare.
Within the self-made confinement, the captive is
inspired by the impressive voices of the past, with the
conviction of words that forever last beyond the chaos,
misunderstandings, and undertakings of a fragile life—
all while longing for rays of warmth from the summer
sun to set upon the lonely, teary face.

Hope Lost

There, between the lines of desolation and destruction,
exists the incoherent blabbing of the destitute.
They search for the elusive answer and solution,
to calm the rough still waters,
and ease the boughs that break the waves
into smooth swatches of foam and debris
carried in from the tumultuous sea.
They continue to seek an uncontrolled yearning
for an outcome not yet written in the expansive sky.
The emptiness of time and space only seems
to embrace the nothingness of the fractured soul.
This being, who cannot be repaired or rehabilitated
into
a productive member of society, who has
long forgotten the fiend or friend.
The lost soul, estranged from the world,
whose nondescript existence is only
accompanied by a lugubrious nature.
This lesser human cannot comprehend the brigand
that has stolen the life source once filled
with exuberant happiness,
as their mind vacillates between the knowledge
and ignorance in the obscurity of spoken words.

Tormented Soul

Mere words cannot describe the complexity of a
tormented soul.
To feel the throngs of deep-seeded pain leaves a
profound path of devastation.
This one who cannot escape the evils that have
followed with unbelievable tenacity
while the tormented struggles to find a ray of hope
and salvation to preserve some essence of human
existence.
Those who surround this human cannot fathom the
wreckage of a life
behind the callous exterior.
No one is allowed to penetrate past the broken shell.
Still within this ravaged heart beats the capacity for
selfless sacrifice and immense compassion for others,
as it seeks to restore the fragile sanity of a life
deprived of normalcy.
The outside world can never see the tear-drenched face
whose loneliness becomes
a curtain of sorrow.
Weakness in the face of such adversity is like death to
the tormented soul.
All must not seek to understand this troubled being,
only to accept the valiance of the battle till the end—
when its light force is reborn to another life, where
there will be peace at last.

Pure & Innocent

The beginning of her life was unstained and unaffected.
She, so small, felt content and protected.
It was all just too fleeting, the happiness, the joy
vanishing and deteriorating like some cosmic ploy.
The demons would find a place to wreak their havoc,
creating devastating years, so long, so tragic.
She, once a pure and innocent young girl,
now brought down by the weight of her world.
She is left shattered, broken, and confused
from being heartbroken, misled, and constantly abused.
On her knees with tear-drenched eyes, she rocks and
sways
as she, now a wearied and worn woman, reverently
prays
and hopelessly waits for her answer.

Broken Heart

There's a place in my heart, once sacred and warm—
now hollowed by those who came, and did me harm.
With every arrival, a promise was made—
yet each departure left deeper the blade.
The damage they caused—to great to repair,
where there was love, there is none—
only remorse and despair.
In place of tenderness, only desperation takes hold,
a darkness more chilling than the loneliest cold.
No longer a haven, my heart lies in fragments,
its beauty reduced to tear-streaked laments.
And so I retreat, shattered and broken,
trapped in the silence, for no words can be spoken.

Beyond the Glass

If only one could see beyond the brilliant rose-colored
window pane
and know that the world is not as it seems or is
portrayed,
but rather a complex matrix joined together in
disillusioned unison;
a beautiful convolution created to confuse the single-
minded human.
Forces in the world indiscriminately remind the weak
that their existence is predicated on false security,
all while the supremacy of the few keeps the normal
human humble and blind to their reality.
So veiled is the lie of disillusion and destruction that no
one's true worth is revealed.
From ever condescending mortals, the innocence of
youth is concealed.
Obscured by the tragedies endured and from humanity
withdrawn,
there in the shadows stands a lesser human begging to
belong.

In the Shadows

There in the shadows, where silence dwells,
I lay beneath the night's mournful spells.
This fight—forsaken, slips from my grasp,
and in defeat I woefully gasp.

If only the dawn, with tender grace,
could find a path to this forsaken place,
with its brilliant light piercing the black,
to guide me forward and bring me back.

Instead the dark creeps into my soul, where voices trail,
through my confused mind and words that fail,
finding no solace for my heart, now torn apart,
its fragile pieces, a broken unspoken art.

The shards lie scattered, cold and bare,
while I anxiously wait in desperate prayer.
For here in this moment the darkness seems to prevail,
though I searched for the light, but to no avail.
Still I dream of a quiet splendorous spark,
to heal my soul and mend my heart.

Resigned to Sadness

Within my fractured state of my mind, dark shadows
rise—
relentless demons invade my fragile thread of sanity.
In the solitude of night, they come,
like villains cloaked in silence, infiltrating my thoughts,
dissolving my clarity.
Those I hold dear— do not truly know
the pain and anguish carved within my soul.
Their hearts are kind, yet blind to the trials I bear,
unable to glimpse the horrors hidden in my silent stare.
Even my prayers seem to go unheard,
as though Heaven itself does not want me to utter
another word.
So I surrender to my fate, here in darkness I remain,
where each falling teardrop becomes a silent reminder
of pain.
I stand alone with only the sounds of my distress,
left to fight the memories I must suppress.
I retreat further into the void, now wearied,
not finding the quiet calming peace I seek.
Here in this forsaken abyss,
I am nothing—nameless, faceless, not to be missed
Hope lies buried beneath sorrow's curtain,
all while my joy fades into the careless air.

When You are Gone

Here in the forsaken night, my darkest fears unveil
while sadness clings with dreams that failed.
Brokenhearted, my tears cascade like rain
no longer able to hide my immeasurable pain.
Alone in this dark and dreary room,
everything feels heavy with dreaded gloom.
My life now unfamiliar and unclear,
While I long for Your voice that is no longer near.
You were my anchor and my guide,
Now I drift wherever the tides decide.
The emptiness grows while my soul fractures
a sentiment that no words can capture.
Your face comes to mind, in a glimpse of light,
slowly diminishing in the forgotten night.
I feel You slipping into faded memory,
as I am left facing my immense agony.
Hopelessly lost now that You're gone,
I search for comfort, but find there is none.

The Darkness Fades

Slowly the curtain of darkness is lifting, no more
sadness to dampen the mood.
The depressing and threatening thoughts no longer
intrude.
The iridescent light is creeping in through the crevices
of my tortured state of mind,
allowing the faint glimmer of hope to enter and find,
a peaceful reprieve from the tumultuous past.
The painful memories are retreating at last.
In anxious resolve, I overcome the fear and overtake
the pain,
no longer doomed to relentless sadness, nor will the
gloom reign.
When the darkness finally fades away, rays of hope
shall take its place.
The new day awaits me with vibrant whispers and a full
embrace.

Brighter Days

In the Silence, in the Darkness

In the silence, I hear the past voices crying out,
creating images of confusion and self-doubt.
In the darkness lay the terrors of a youth denied,
leaving me speechless with nowhere to hide.
Like fleeting ghosts beneath my skin,
they claw at my fragile state from within.
In shadows deep, the demons reach,
their fingers cold, their words impeach,
fighting a vexatious battle, scarred by horrendous acts
imposed
never to be unveiled, never to be exposed.
The chaos prevents my mind from blocking out the
insanity.
Still, the power inside increases, shaking off the
inhumanity.
No longer do I fear the perplexing words they say.
Frightened, lonely, and confused, still I make my way
toward the rays of light and hope—freed from the pain
to end my suffering's strangling reign,
finding a peaceful realm where my persistent past
will no longer haunt me—it ends at last!

Troubled Soul

What a troubled soul lies deep within me,
Not knowing where to go, yet longing to be free
From all of life's hardships, especially the pain.
Of losing old friendships—now memories remain.
But how to go on believing
There may be a better road ahead,
When so many things are deceiving
And others are hard to comprehend.
Still the answers sought are hidden inside,
and not always easy to find.
So I won't let my conscience misguide me—
For they're locked in my heart not my mind.

Desperate for an Answer

Tears falling endlessly,
surrounded by darkness, not a trace of light.
Locked away in a sanctuary of quiet,
the desperate soul seeks solutions.
Overwhelmed by impossible situations,
hopelessly lost in a world of dismay,
wandering without a word to say.
Found by today with more to endure
with thoughts of no possible or probable cure.
Troubled by many, answered by none,
abandoned, it seems by everyone.
Thus the closed mind with closed eyes
does not consciously realize—
the answer walks in only if the door is open.

Rise up, be Unbroken

From tumbled heights, you fall into a perilous plot
devised by your mind to create a false illusion.
In the dark shadows of your mind, you are deep in
thought,
trying to make sense of the chaos and confusion.
Life has been brutally cruel and unfair.
You yearn for relief from this existence, but it is not
there.
It hurts to move into the sunbeams, to grasp at hope.
At this moment, there is no strength to cope.
You lift your head to the skies and cry
without knowing or understanding the reasons why.
At this moment, you search for help but none is found.
You are battered and broken, deeply distressed on the
ground.
Then suddenly, the light reveals that the unbroken
pieces will heal
when you lower your head and purposefully kneel.
In silent prayer, the answers come,
whispers inspiring you—now it's time to rise up
and be unbroken!

Where I Don't Belong

In this callous world filled with people who can't
understand my soul,
they fail to see the victor inside this mess of a being.
I have come to an acceptance that I will never fit in the
proverbial round hole.
My mind is made of so many conflicting memories and
thoughts,
making it hard to see the positive sides of life.
The clouds hide the light and create the darkness I
face.
From the floor, I rise to meet the challenge of the day.
No one will stop my progress, no one will squash my
resolve
here in this place I don't belong, pained by the
thoughtlessness
of the people who surround me.
Someday there will be a place where my heart aches no
more, my tears subside, and the scars are healed.
Until that day, I stand still but do not yield,
for my strength is coming.

Rare Pearl

There, hidden beneath the veil of darkness,
tucked away, is the lustrous precious gem
who must wait to see the light of day.
Once the splendor of this beauty appears,
the world will take notice with wonder and awe.
How could such a treasure exist in the midst of chaos?
Created through years of harsh environments
only to appear as a rare pearl, whose radiance shines
upon the world,
once the calloused shell is discarded.

"Resilient people aren't born, they are made by the struggles they face, the challenges they overcome, and the tenacity to keep pushing forward. And even still, they have the audacity to think they can change the world." –Margie Westmoreland

Pretty Moon

Rise up from your broken and shattered past.
Know that the hardships in life never last.
Fight through the immeasurable pain and be strong,
even when all things seem to be going wrong.
Even when dark shadows loom within the crevices of
your mind,
reminding you of all the things you left behind.
Even when confusion closes in on your sanity—
surrounded only by the veils of your created agony.
Listen for the sound of hope in the whispery air,
look for the rays of valiant triumph, if you dare.
Then, rise—
like the pretty moon that rises against the gloomy
darkness,
unsure of what awaits in the murky shadows of sadness.
It shines forth with brilliant splendor to illuminate the
sky.
Leave the past in buried memory, never questioning
why.
Though the morning threatens to deny your sparkle,
choose to be a courageous unrelenting mortal
shining forth into your new reclaimed tomorrow.
No glancing back at yesterday's heartache and sorrow.
Choose to rise up and show the world your internal
light
and finally make the harrowing wrongs irrevocably
right.

The Champion Inside

You my past, how you have tortured me,
ever present in my mind, threatening my sanity.
You tried to drag my soul into the dark abyss,
never to be found, never to be missed.
I fought against my fatal thoughts,
wrought with pain and anguish.
I wrestled with the voices telling me I wasn't worthy,
not even worth the breath existing in my body,
which led me to question why I was living.
Just when all hope seemed lost forever
I pulled my wearied body from the cold hard floor,
as I shouted to the demons in my mind, "You will
torment me no more!"

Open Window

With the curtain pulled back, allowing the sunlight to cascade
upon my weathered, wearied face,
it is time to view the world in a different shade of blue.
One reminiscent of the ocean's calming hue.
No more weeping while struggling to get out of bed.
No more hopeless thoughts percolating around in my head.
It is time for acceptance of a life less than defined.
One to be forgotten, to be forever enshrined,
in the furthest region of my mind.
For when the past is laid to rest, my soul can take flight,
where no darkness exists, only the brilliance of light.

Character

A path unfolds and trials arise,
a choice awaits in the shadowed skies;
to stand, to break, to push, to fall
yet still, the choice is ours, through it all.
To give excuses a voice, soft yet strong,
giving in to defeated thoughts and a sorrowed song;
or forge ahead with strong resolve and fearless might,
and carve a dream in the new morning light.
For dreams do not just fall away and die,
unless we let them drift and pass us by.
They rest within us, and remain,
until we call them forth again.

Broken Butterflies

Broken butterflies may never soar,
but they crawl, they climb, they reach for more.
Wings torn, yet hearts unbowed,
they fight against the raging cloud.
In silent pain, they carry on,
fragile, yet fierce, though hope seems gone.
They cannot fly, but still they rise,
proving strength behind weary eyes.

The wind may threaten, cruel and wild,
yet they cling to life defiled,
survival etched into their frame,
refusing loss, defying shame—
escaping shadows of the past,
growing stronger, standing fast.

Like broken butterflies, I crawl, I climb,
chasing the stars, grasping time.
No storm can steal what I possess,
no struggle will my dreams suppress.
I am torn, I am broken, yet still alive,
and like the butterfly—I will survive.

Path of Reflection

Beyond the clearing, a path unfolds,
where a quiet place the earth beholds.
A reprieve from my misery,
where the painful memories fade away,
where regret and remorse dare not stay.
There the tall pines canopy my thoughts,
while shielding my weeping eyes
and the wind whisks away my worries in its breeze
Fear and doubt lose all their weight,
for here in nature, I find a kinder fate.
Memories may linger, while shadows cast,
yet here I stand without the past;
a sacred space to breathe, to mend,
to trust that my pain is near the end.
Through trembling prayers, I come to see,
that I am not alone—He walks with me.
In His presence, I reclaim,
the strength to rise, and shed my shame.

Buried Wings, Rising Dreams

In the red-clay dirt, I knelt alone,
burying wings that once had flown,
a fragile little life was lost.
The fateful day our paths did cross.
The world was cruel, my sky was dim,
yet somewhere hope still stirred within.
No shattered past would cage my soul,
no broken fate would take control.
I was more than sorrow's weight,
more than fear, more than fate.
A small-town girl with fire inside,
with dreams too vast, too fierce to hide.
Never slowing down, never looking back,
finding strength where light once lacked.
In my child's eyes, I saw my way,
I made a promise for a brighter day.
Through every storm, I called His name,
for courage, grace, and his to claim.

A Brilliant Destiny

The pain is slowly healing, deep within my heart and
mind,
the light of hope now flickers bright, a way to start and
to shine;
to make the clouds of sorrow fade, to chase away the
past,
to shape a world where joy remains, where light is
meant to last.
Though the harm was done, it cannot change the
strength I hold inside;
that the voices of the past are quieted, I no longer have
to hide.
It's time to rebuild my dreams, to rise anew, to cast my
grief away,
to silence all the screaming thoughts and never let them
stay
For now I step into tomorrow's call—its promise shining
strong,
no more regrets, no turning back, just moving forward
on;
for life awaits, so brilliant and so bold,
a fashioned fate created just for me,
an unshakable, remarkable, and brilliant destiny.

Shells of Youth Betrayed

The waves of the past sometimes wash over the echoes in my mind,
daring me to forget—to leave the darkness behind.
Tortured through my youth, I felt scared and betrayed,
wondering why I had not left, instead I stayed.
My life's outlook was only dreary
no focus, just lost alone, battered, and teary.
Still something inside seemed to call—
a voice that couldn't be silenced,
asking me to look for the resolutions for a life less defined.
It beckoned me to stand against the currents of self-doubt,
to break the shackles of sadness and create a way out,
this time finding the courage and strength needed to succeed
for the future is waiting, now that I'm freed!

Infinite Symphony of Freedom

The battle between my scarred past and my destined
future
continues to wage war inside my mind;
a never-ending chaos that exists to challenge,
confuse, and yet encourage me.

As I seek a way out of the shadows that consume my
thoughts,
the hope that waits for me is just beyond the looming
horizon
—within reach, within my grasp, I leap forward with
exuberant determination and power.

Patiently standing with an awakened sense of self,
it's my time, it's my hour.
Hearing only the melodic sounds of victory,
I now move toward the iridescent light,
where no darkness will overshadow my incredible
might.

The days that follow belong to the courageous human
being hidden
for far too long in the murky hell of my existence,
where I was met with hatred, harm, and resistance.

Now liberated from the chains of isolation, rejection,
and self-loathing
no longer a prisoner, at long last I am living.

The Light Shines Forth

The darkness has now lifted, and the radiant light pours across my face,
no longer tethered to my sorrow, joy blooms just beyond the horizon.

Hope waits in the brilliance of what lies ahead in a recreated future,
my destiny shaped by the strength that carried me through every tribulation.

And though the scars are forever carved into my story, they remind me of the faith and strong spirit that lived within me.
Now no longer a prisoner to my ill-fated past,
I carry on like a true warrior.

And as I rise from the remnants of what once tried to break me, a new chapter is waiting to be written in the fortuitous days ahead.

The same light that found me now guides my steps, leading me toward the next triumph truth waiting to be told.

Into the Light

I Dared to Be Great!

I dared to be great so that I might overcome
the torturous oppression and dastardly beasts
that bound me to a lesser existence.
I fought hard to reclaim my self-image and pride
as I stood alone at the crossroads of life
with no one in whom to confide.

I grew stronger with each insurmountable obstacle
that rose in my way.
And even when the most tempting solution
was to surrender in dismay,
I held fast, climbed higher, dug deeper,
and escaped the oppression I once endured.
Though my body grew weary and tired,
my soul knew it must prevail.

I dared to be great so that my greatness
might overshadow your tears and shortcomings,
sparking a resplendent light of hope
as you hold fast to the life-sustaining rope—
the one that lifts you to a higher plane of understanding
and helps you become more than you believed you
could be.
So you would not know discouragement, but find
comfort
in knowing you will always be with me—
for it is because of you, my children,
that I dared to be great.

* * First published in an anthology "Collected Whispers" copyright
2008 by International Library of Poetry as a compilation.

This is Who I Am

I am a troubled and complex soul,
but with a simple plan in mind,
and determination to achieve my ultimate goal,
leaving all my troubles far behind.
My past is but a faded memory
where all demons are lost and
all thoughts of hopelessness fade away
as I turn toward the inspired future
where there are no regrets and excuses,
no barriers or impossibilities exist.
All the curious faces who do not know
the horrors I have lived through
stand in judgment of my choices
and criticize everything I do.
They do not seem to understand
that I don't need anyone to validate me
or tell me who I should or should not be.
If people could see what I am made of
they would see a person made of courage, resilience,
and faith—
a soul saved by God's love!

My Soul-Healing Ritual

Here I sit in the corner of the half-lit room,
waiting for my creative spirit to bloom,
as my greatest thoughts are being realized into words.
Settling into my moment of passion, my inspiration
stirs.
There are no obstacles standing in my way,
no one to tear my lofty dreams away,
only visualizing my internal ponderings and writing
the prose of the day.
Should a distraction come along to throw me off
course,
I will look for the influence of years past and present
to keep me on task, I suppose.
In the quietude of night, my thoughts are expanding
the verbiage of language, I am commanding.
With resilient resolve, I create
whatever future I desire as my fate.

Finding My Peace

Once, my life was so vivid, so bright—
faded to shadows in the dark of night.
Time etched wounds upon my soul,
fractured dreams no longer whole.
Adrift, forsaken, and seeking reprieve,
I was lost in shaded memory, forced to grieve.
Yet, within the depths of sorrow's art,
a quiet strength embraced my heart.
Through trials fierce, through storms untamed,
I rose, unbroken, though scarred and maimed.
No more silence, no more despair,
no more worries, no more cares.
Though healing bore a heavy toll,
it freed the weight upon my soul.
Now unafraid, I stand released—
embraced by light, adorned in peace.

Capable

I am capable—strong and sure;
 to move the mountains, to endure,
 to rise above the trials steep,
 to chase the dreams I long to keep.
I am capable—bold and bright;
 to turn the darkness into light,
 to challenge norms, to shift the way,
 to build tomorrow from today.
I am capable—my dreams ignite;
 to guide my plans, to set them right,
 to change the world, to shape, to mold,
 to make a future strong and bold.
And most of all, I stand unshaken,
 for love is found where hope was taken.
 The hardest road, the steepest climb,
 brings the greatest gift in God's time.

A Purposeful Plan

God's will, though often shrouded in mystery, is never without intention. I grapple with the meaning of my existence, questioning the purpose behind my birth, yet here I stand—breathing, enduring, becoming. My blessings are abundant, yet sorrow lingers, a shadow casting itself over my joys, as the tears continue to fall. I long for wholeness, yet find myself unraveling. I yearn for strength, though moments of profound weakness threaten to consume me. Hope beckons from the horizon, yet today feels impossibly heavy. The memories I wish to cherish slip through my fingers as time accelerates, moving far too swiftly. I desire to embrace life, yet I know the hands of fate will determine when my time must cease.

Still, while I remain in this world, I must honor the gifts I have been given. I must wield them with purpose, weaving inspiration into the lives of others, letting my light shine through the darkness—because even amid sorrow, even through uncertainty, I now know there is a reason for my existence.

Without Restriction

My soul is boundless, untethered, free.
The past no longer holds me captive,
its weight slipping from my grasp.
My heart longs for healing,
for the brilliance of redemption,
for the triumph that awaits beyond the shadows.
I step forward, unwavering,
toward the light of victory,
refusing to accept anything
less than the dreams I have envisioned.
I will not be confined by yesterday's chains,
though forever changed by their lessons.
I will rise without restriction,
defining my path,
becoming all that I was meant to be.
Unbound.
Limitless.
Whole.

The Power Within

The shadows of the past trample through my mind,
creeping in when I least expect them. I fight to push
back the tears, to bury the wounds in the furthest
depths of my recall, yet they refuse to retreat. They
linger, reminding me that nothing in life comes without
a cost—a toll to be paid in hardship, in struggle, and in
pain. And yet, within that suffering, something
extraordinary has taken shape.

I emerge full of hope and possibilities. I am not merely
the remnants of what I have endured.
I am the product of perseverance, sculpted by battles
won and lost, marked by scars that speak of resilience.

The world has tried to break me, but here I stand,
gathering the fragments of my shattered life, piecing
myself back together with strength and dignity.

I escaped life's insidious snare. Now looking back, I see
the path I have walked, the trials that threatened to
destroy me, and I exhale knowing my time has finally
come.

No longer will I remain in the shadows, for I am a
fighter, and my journey is proof of the hardships I have
overcome. With unwavering determination, I carve my
way through the chaos, through the heartbreak and
solitude, and through the violence and hatred.

I made it through everything that dared to stand between me and the life I was meant to live. My cries for help and my constant prayers finally reaching heaven, have rescued me.

Now, at last, a soul is redeemed, a heart is healed, a dream is realized. The power within me has conquered the demons of my past, the harm inflicted upon me, the pain that stretched across decades, feeling like an eternity. And though the scars remain, they do not define me.

I am healed.
I am whole.
I am—forever me.

Where Peace Lives

Everyday offers the chance to start anew
but every night I must wrestle with my tortured past.
My life feels heavy when I remember the agony, the
pain.
Each teardrop holds the weight of my emotions—
joy and sorrow, frustration and love,
a silent testament to all I have endured.
But the day has come for my tears to cease,
for anguish to dissolve into quiet serenity,
for my spirit to find a place untouched by chaos and
confusion.
Here, all dreams are possible.
The voices no longer question my strength.
I stand not as a captive creature of yesterday,
but as the courageous creator of my own story.
No longer bound by sadness and fear,
no longer imprisoned by shadows of doubt,
I rise, unburdened and free—
soaring toward my determined destiny,
forever at peace.

Your New Day is Here

Today you must emerge strong from shadow's hold,
your worth is now known, your story waiting to be told.
No longer bound by dreadful doubt or crippling pain,
the time has come to fight and rise once again.
Do not let your sorrow stake its claim,
nor let past wounds call out your name.
Stand tall, press forward, and lift your gaze,
while you embrace the light of brighter days.
As night dissolves into sunlight's golden hue,
the world unfolds, refreshed and new.
The road ahead is yours to steer,
bold and steady—your new day is here.

Just be You

Do not let the weight of hardship harden your
incredible heart or detour your destiny.
Let it forge you into something greater and stronger
than you thought you could be.
Dare to dream boldly and build the life you envisioned.
Do not surrender to the reverberations of the past.
Heal, even when it hurts,
for pain unchecked will tether you to darkness.
Forgive, even those who have wounded you,
for hatred, if left to continue, can consume and leaves
no room for love.
There will be moments when words fail,
when silence speaks louder than sound.
Listen to the voices of wisdom
guiding you toward all that lies ahead.
You are battle-worn, but unbroken.
You are scarred, yet undeniably resilient.
You are a masterpiece of endurance,
a painfully crafted creation.
So step forward with new-found courage, rise with
exuberant strength, and just be you.

Phoenix Moon

As sleep eludes me, I lie awake, my mind brimming
with hope and wonder. The quiet pull of the midnight
hour beckons, and I slip out into the embrace of the
night. Above me, my steadfast companion—the
luminous yellow moon—casts its familiar glow,
unchanged by the passing of time. Yet I am not as I
once was.

I have endured the weight of countless obstacles,
navigated arduous trials, and weathered tribulations that
threatened to break me. And from that crucible of
transformation, I have emerged reborn—a being shaped
by struggle, strengthened by perseverance. Beneath this
celestial beacon, I stand renewed, like the Phoenix
rising from the ashes, my spirit soaring into the vast
expanse of possibility.

The future beckons me to emit my own radiance and
shine forth with renewed determination and humble
valiance.

Metamorphosis of My Soul

Inside the warm vessel of my existence,
I could hide in the shadows from all who try to do me
harm,
yet there was no way to escape my snare.
There was no one to save me, or even to care.
Alone in the darkness, I fought to stay alive.
I had to withstand the struggle; I had to survive.
Within my dysfunctional world, I faced mounting
difficulties.
My mind was plagued with anxiousness and endless
worries.
The past gone, I emerged triumphant with a fierce
mentality.
Finally free from my painful youth, I was awakened to a
renewed vitality—
a steel resolve no one could penetrate or even shatter.
Most people couldn't understand my complex story,
but that didn't matter.
I was no longer alone; I had what I needed to withstand
any storm.
I am now a victorious warrior, a fighter in the rarest of
form;
my determined wings ready to take flight into the
unknown,
moving forward into a future life, the one I make my
own.

Listening

I know You listen to my pleas.
You know the pain I have endured.
You know what my shattered heart needs.
And even though I failed You so many times in this life,
You heard my cries of anguish.
Consumed with grief, in my darkest hours, You found me;
broken, afraid, and lost.
Still, I held on to my faith no matter what the costs.
In the shadows of my mind, You showed me the light,
the beacon for this miserable human's plight.
I do not think of my character as flawed, but rather
as stormed and weathered by the evils of the past,
remembering that the most harrowing moments never last.
These ragged reminders in the cobwebs of my mind
keep me humbled and will not let me forget that
the road ahead is better than the one I left behind.
I do not need people to accept me, approve of me, pity me,
or even to understand who I am—through the insanity.
I have learned to come to terms with this woman
ravaged by social ills,
who has become stronger like a warrior in victory,
carrying forever the scars of the battles I faced.
But always at peace because I know You are still listening.

Heaven's Light

Through the depths of heartache, I found the strength
to move forward.
Every obstacle no longer brings me fear, nor do I dread
tomorrow.

No longer a prisoner, I am the victor over this chaotic
life I was living.
Whole again, restored by grace, I stand unburdened
and forgiven.

With every wound, every sorrow redeemed, and from
ruin, I have risen.
The faith that once wavered within now illuminates my
path,
driving away the darkness that long held me in its wrath.

Painful memories no longer define me, nor does fateful
misery.
With solid resolve guided by purpose and light, the
future waits for me;
ready to share my story—my suffering, my gift, and my
victory.

Renewed by divine love, I hold within me all I need to
take the next step;
to move away from the past, shedding the weight of
pain and regret.

Yesterday, I was fraught with sorrow far too great to
withstand alone.

Today, I am scarred but unbroken and no longer on
my own.

Tomorrow, I shall rise stronger, prepared to embrace
my destiny—
my mind uncluttered with visions of clarity.

Each day, I will forge ahead without shackles of
affliction or chains of shame;
until my resilient journey ends and heaven lovingly calls
my name.

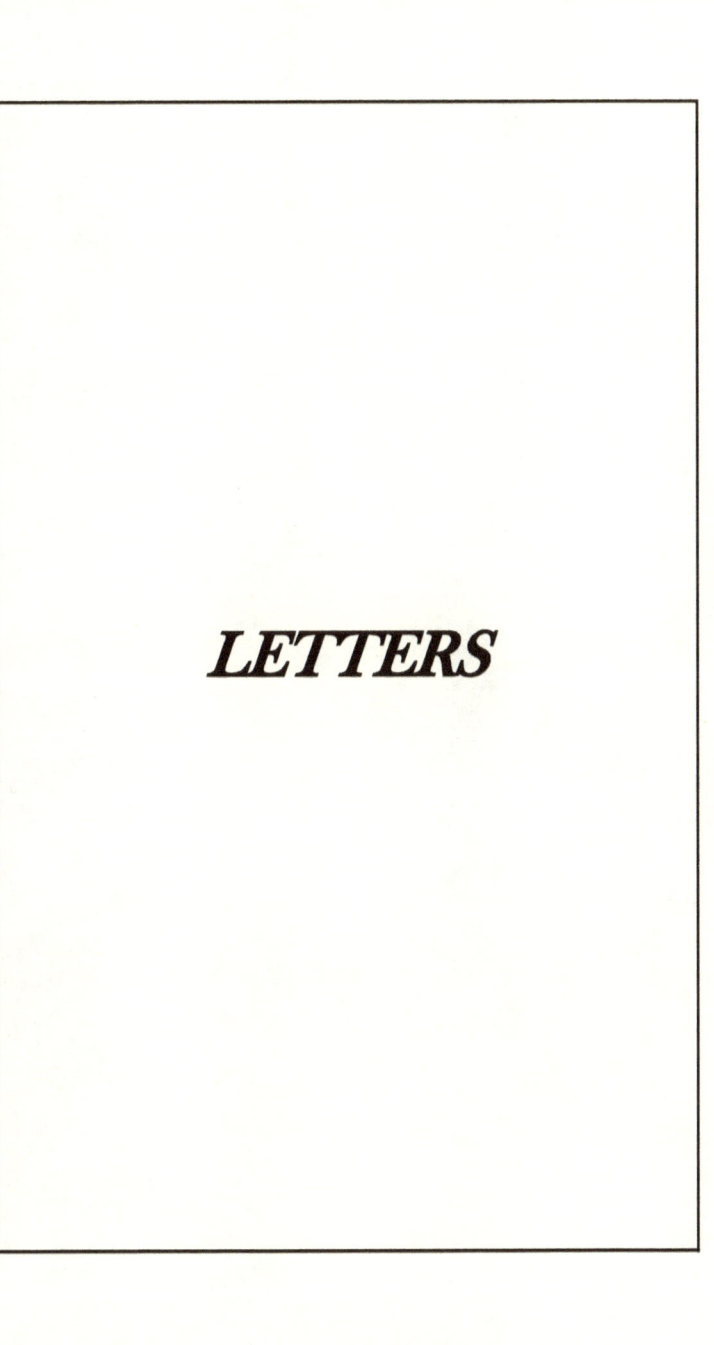

LETTERS

Unspoken Words

When words failed me, I wrote my thoughts on paper
or typed them into my computer. These letters carried
the weight of what my voice could not hold, capturing
the truths that trembled on my tongue. In ink and
keystrokes, I found a language for my silence, a way to
speak even when I could not be heard.

A Letter to My Child

There are things that words sometimes struggle to carry, but today, I write with a heart full of hope, truth, and unwavering love.

From the very beginning, you've been my guiding light. Through life's storms and shadows, your existence gave me the strength to hold on. My past was marked by hardship—tragedies that felt as familiar as breathing—but somehow, through it all, I survived. And I did so for you.

Education wasn't just a path to a better job for me—it was my lifeline. It helped me reclaim my life when everything felt broken. That's why I speak so passionately about its importance. Not because I want to shape your future to match my own, but because I believe education can be the springboard to discovering your purpose, just as it was for me.

You see the world with eyes that grasp far more than most. That depth within you is rare, and I've always known you are meant to forge your own way—not someone's version of success. Support doesn't mean control. When I encourage you, it's not because I need you to fulfill my dreams. It's because I see greatness within you, and I want you to realize it for yourself.

I've asked God for guidance countless times, and I believe you are here for a reason. I may not know what that reason is, but I trust you'll find it.

Please know this: no matter where life takes you, I will always believe in you, stand beside you, and love you beyond anything this world can measure. You are my greatest accomplishment, my deepest pride, and my forever joy.

With all my love,
Your Parent

A Letter to Humankind

I'm writing to you tonight because I've been reflecting on everything that has occurred in my life.

Thinking about the analysis of logical reasoning versus emotional rationalization, I came to the realization that what sets man apart from the animals and other creatures is the ability to feel different emotions.

All decisions cannot be based on logic or reasoning. Why do we even feel love, if we are not going to give it the voice it deserves? To ignore this voice of love is the most tragic deed of all.

To love is not and will never be wrong. To regret that which the heart feels is to regret what we are.

Maybe I am a hopeless romantic, but I believe in love's power.

Love can transform the human heart, overcome all obstacles or tragedies, give hope to a lonely heart, and give life to a dying soul, but above all that it can endure even in death because it knows no boundaries or limits.

I am a person with a lot of love to give to those who will accept unconditional but pure love.

I want to be someone who somehow made a difference in this world, to contribute to the betterment of humanity.

I want to be someone who made someone's life better
because they knew me, because I was their family,
a friend, a co-worker, a compassionate stranger, or just
because I made them smile.

We should all strive to be better human beings and to
love more, even when we think we cannot.
One day I hope to touch people through my poetic and
romantic words.

Having said all this, I wish you well. Do not forget—
your ability to love is the most powerful force on earth!

A Letter to Father Tim

As a member of your church, I want you to know that I am truly listening—not just hearing your words. As I watch you deliver the Word of God, I often wonder if you realize that while our congregation may be present in body, not all are not fully engaged in spirit.

As an educator, I understand how difficult it can be to capture and maintain my students' attention. I often question whether my efforts are making a meaningful difference in their lives, as my goal is to change the world, one student at a time. However, before I could impact others, I had to first change myself.

My life didn't begin easily; it was filled with tribulations, disasters, and hardships. Yet, I persevered through these challenges. Through my experiences, I have learned that life without God is not truly living. He can only work through us if we are willing to look deep within ourselves and confront the shortcomings that we, as humans, possess. It is a challenge to continually remind ourselves of our imperfections.

We have the capacity to improve as parents, children, teachers, and church members, but most importantly, as children of God. We, humankind, should not be disconnected from the community we share. It is disheartening to recognize that our society with its flaws often resists efforts to improve this world we live in.

The reason I am writing to you is that, as a teacher, it gives me purpose to know that at least one child has listened to me. I want you to know that I hear you with my ears, my mind, and my heart. God assures us that we are fulfilling our calling when we truly believe His words, but only then can we hear Him speaking to our spirit.

The Writer

This is me, the writer.

Today marks the beginning of another day. I am uncertain about what it will bring, whether it will present challenges, changes, unexpected surprises, or simply be an ordinary day. What I do know is that I must write; it is an integral part of who I am. As far back as I can remember, I have been writing. For me, not writing creates a sense of longing. Something compels me to put words down on the page, as if they need to be expressed for me to truly survive. Becoming a published author who has reached and perhaps healed others, would be a dream realized, but for now, I will keep writing and allow the words and phrases to heal my soul. Throughout my life, I have met many people, yet no one truly understands the complexities of the thoughts that percolate in my mind. I often feel like I'm trying to fit into a round hole with my square edges. To stifle my need to write or create prose is to restrict the very essence of my life. Words are like oxygen to me; without them, I don't feel alive—I can't breathe. I refuse to succumb to a slow death, devoid of meaningful lexicon. Today and forever, I must write.

It Is Your Turn to Shine

Go out into the world—
don't let anyone diminish your light.
Tomorrow is yours to mold
into the vision of what your life can become.

Leave the demons in the past.
Push forward
with incredible might.

The hopeful future belongs
to those who dare
to overcome adversity,
to rise from tragedy.

The scars of your past
are not defeat.
They are proof:

You are a survivor.
You are a warrior.
You are a rare human—
with dreams to realize.

Final Words from the Author

"The darkness eventually fades away if you look for the light to guide your way." – Margie Westmoreland

These poems were a labor of many years, decades of working through my shattered life. The prose and mood changed as I changed. These lines and verses evolved as I crafted a better place for myself in this world.

For those who have read the ramblings of this weathered soul, may you find comfort in those things that bring you peace. Grace only comes when we are forced to evaluate how much God cares for us and carries us through the most difficult times in our lives.

Know that there will be storms in your life but with each passing one, you will become stronger. Let the pain guide you to a purposeful plan—a plan designed and divinely guided just for you.

"'For I know the plans I have for you,' declares the Lord, 'plans to prosper you and not to harm you, plans to give you hope and a future." – Jeremiah 29:11.

About The Author

Dr. Margie Westmoreland holds a PhD in Educational Administration from Mississippi State University. A lifelong writer, she began crafting poetry at the age of thirteen, using words as a refuge and a means to reflect on the complexities of life. Her work—both poetry and prose—is inspired by real experiences and rooted in the resilience of the human spirit. With honesty and hope at the core of her storytelling, Dr. Westmoreland writes for those navigating hardship, searching for healing, or yearning to break free from difficult circumstances.

Her poetry has been published, recognized, and selected as a semi-finalist in the International Library of Poetry. Her poetry has also been recognized by fellow readers for its emotional depth and authenticity. She has self-published this collection, her debut book, through her own company, Rising Hope Publishing, and continues to work on future projects that aim to uplift and inspire. Her voice is one of quiet strength, her stories and poems a lifeline for those still finding their way.